BONSAI

The Ultimate Beginner's Guide on How To Cultivate, Take Care and Grow Your Bonsai Tree (Ideal for Any Bonsai Type | #2020 Version)

Riku Nishimura

Legal & Disclaimer

The information contained in this book and its contents is not designed to replace or take the place of any form of medical or professional advice; and is not meant to replace the need for independent medical, financial, legal or other professional advice or services, as may be required. The content and information in this book has been provided for educational and entertainment purposes only.

The content and information contained in this book has been compiled from sources deemed reliable, and it is accurate to the best of the Author's knowledge, information and belief. However, the Author cannot guarantee its accuracy and validity and cannot be held liable for any errors and/or omissions. Further, changes are periodically made to this book as and when needed. Where appropriate and/or necessary, you must consult a professional (including but not limited to your doctor, attorney, financial advisor or such other professional advisor) before using any of the suggested remedies, techniques, or information in this book.

Upon using the contents and information contained in this book, you agree to hold harmless the Author from and against any damages, costs, and expenses, including any legal fees potentially resulting from the application of any of the information provided by this book. This disclaimer applies to any loss, damages or injury caused by the use and application, whether directly or indirectly, of any advice or information presented, whether for breach of contract, tort, negligence, personal injury, criminal intent, or under any other cause of action.

You agree to accept all risks of using the information presented inside this book.

You agree that by continuing to read this book, where appropriate and/or necessary, you shall consult a professional (including but not limited to your doctor, attorney, or financial advisor or such other advisor as needed) before using any of the suggested remedies, techniques, or information in this book.

Table of Contents

Introduction

I would like to thank you for downloading this book, "Bonsai: The ultimate beginners guide on how to cultivate and take care of your bonsai tree."

Do you want to know how to grow bonsai trees? How to select them and how to take care of them? Do you want to learn more about the tools you will need, and all the other basics? If your answer is yes, then you have chosen the right book!

A bonsai can be any tree that is grown in miniature using artistic techniques so it resembles an aged tree. The value of a bonsai depends on its maturity. The more mature it is, the more its potential value. You can grow different kinds of trees and train them to be bonsais. Bonsai is the Japanese word for a tree grown in a container. However, it doesn't mean that you can just place a tree in a pot and expect it to be a bonsai. You need to patiently train the tree's foliage and guide it into the desired shape. You have to prune the roots to keep the tree small, wire its branches, and use other techniques to let the tree mature into a bonsai. It requires intimate care!

While learning the art of bonsai, the plethora of information out there can seem quite overwhelming. What kind of plant do you choose? How do you take care of it? How much water will it need?

What about the container size? How would you prune it and so on and so forth? In this concise book, you will learn everything you need to know to grow your bonsai. So, why don't we get started?

Chapter 1: What is Bonsai?

History of bonsai

Bonsai are trees and plants that are grown in containers where their whole beauty is captured in miniature. It's an ancient technique that can be traced back to the Han Dynasty around 206 BC-220 AD. The earliest reference to bonsai as we know it today dates back to a poem from the mid-fourteenth century. However, the widespread usage didn't start until three centuries later. Pictures of bonsai are seen in scrolls that date back to 1309. This ancient practice can indeed make a person forget about their stresses and rejoice in the serenity that a simple bonsai offers.

During ancient times, bonsais were reserved for the delight of aristocrats, priests, and high-ranking individuals. It was during the seventeenth century that ordinary people started to take pleasure in them. Japan opened itself up to the western world after almost three centuries of isolation in 1868. Once it did, bonsais came to be recognized as an art form and people began to grow bonsai as a hobby. At present, bonsai-growing is a hobby that many enjoy and is a significant part of Japan's art and culture.

Caring for bonsais isn't just a Japanese pastime anymore. In 1989, a World Bonsai Convention in Omiya saw more than 1200 people from 32 different countries attend the event. It goes to show the enthusiasm that people have for bonsai.

Developing and cultivating bonsai is an artistic hobby. You don't need to have a green thumb to grow bonsai; you just need practice, skill and patience. Bonsai is an excellent example of the gentle respect that the Japanese have for all living things! It requires significantly more care and commitment than a regular potted plant.

There is little restriction on the kind of plants or tree that can be turned into bonsai. Theoretically, any plant can be grown in a small container as a bonsai. The most popular options for bonsai are pines, maples, flowering trees like cherry or plum, and several other fruit-bearing trees. A bonsai is as tall as three feet or even small enough to fit in one's palm. Bonsai's can be categorized depending on the shape and structure of the plant.

Common Curiosities for Bonsai

You can grow bonsai from a seed

If you really want to get the full experience of growing bonsai, you may consider starting from a seed. For those who are really committed to the process, this is much more appealing than purchasing a fully-grown bonsai then maintaining it. Of course, growing bonsai from a seed is both time-consuming and challenging. But it is more rewarding in terms of the experience you will gain from the whole process. Just make sure that you purchase the bonsai seed from a reputable source and choose the seed(s) carefully.

Buying fully-grown bonsai is more common for beginners

For those who would like to have their own bonsai, but don't think that they can grow one successfully, they have the option to purchase a plant that is already fully-grown. For such a case, you should purchase your plant from specialist bonsai growers to ensure that you're getting the best one for yourself. Do research on which shops offer fully-grown bonsai in your locale before you make a final choice.

Many people consider bonsai as an investment

Whether you plan to grow bonsai from seed or maintain a fully-grown one, you need to invest a lot of time and care into it. Think of your bonsai as an investment and the more you put into it, the more rewarding it becomes. If you're one who wants quick results, then you may want to find a different hobby.

Repotting bonsai isn't a one-time thing

As you will later on discover, it's vital to continue repotting your bonsai as it grows in vigor and size. As you see your bonsai flourish, you should re-pot it as needed. Changing your bonsai's pot is also important for its overall health and growth. Without this step, you might be hindering your bonsai from reaching its true potential.

Chapter 2: Different style of bonsai plants

Formal upright or Chokkan style

This style is characterized by the presence of a single trunk which grows gradually tapering towards the apex in the classical conical shape. Here the succession of the branches departing from the trunk is fundamental: starting from the base of the trunk, there must be a first branch, the most robust one, placed on one side for the onlooker. The second branch must be a little smaller than the first and placed just above the first branch on the opposite side; the third branch must be still smaller and placed above the second branch but on the opposite side and so forth each time reducing the branches in size forming an ideal conical shape up to the top. As in Moyogi style, the branches will grow horizontal to the ground or slightly downward (to simulate the weight of the years). The species that are best suited to this style are the young conifers that can still be educated and straightened: in fact the natural winding tendency of the shaft is difficult to recover in older plants.

Informal upright or Moyogi style

The informal upright style is the one that comes closest to the natural winding tendency of the trees. The vertical of the trunk is perfectly straight, but the silhouette of the torso bends according to functional logics that make the plant more aged and real. As for the Chokkan style, the branches are always randomly alternated, but always on the outside of the curves (in nature branches that extend from the inside of a curve do not exist).

The first branch is always the largest, while the other are reduced in size as they approach the apex. The species that are best suited to this style are: Oak, Pine, Hornbeam, Elm and Beech. If a young plant does not have these winding features, you can shape its silhouette with wiring and pruning. Be careful with pruning not to weaken the plant; you must eliminate only the bulky branches at the apex of the trunk according to the theory that the thicker and longer branches are found only at the base (because they are older) while the smaller ones are at the apex (because they are younger).

Tilted or Shakan style

In this style, the vertical is not aligned and the apex is tilted to one side of the base: the branches alternate on both sides as in previous styles. Here though the first branch must always grow in the opposite direction to that of the inclination of the trunk.

Of particular value in this style is the presence of exposed roots that emphasize the "will" of the tree to remain anchored to the ground. This style is fairly easy to create if you start with small seedlings, but difficult if you use an already developed tree.

Growing in a rock or Ishitsuki style

This style is formed by a tree that grows in a niche in a rock constituting a whole; the roots cling to the rock reaching down to the soil. To create this style the main roots must be exposed and cleaned from the soil. Then you select a suitable rock where to place your Bonsai and fill a niche with the appropriate soil. You firmly anchor the Bonsai to the rock and place the now joined Bonsai and rock in a larger container. The roots will have to be covered up to the base of the trunk. As the roots grow, you will gradually remove the soil uncovering the roots.

These will show the strength of the tree and its will to survive even in the most hostile environments. Water and fertilize with care given the little soil available. The best suited plants for this style are: Pine, Fir, Serissa, Ficus.

Chapter 3: Different types of bonsai plants

Flowering crabapple

Most apple species does well when used for bonsai most especially the crabapple. The crabapple is mostly preferred to other any other apple specie due to its amazing beauty. it does perfectly well when used for bonsai. the crabapple can also be shaped into different styles of bonsai.

Pomegranate

Furkien tea

This is a topiocal tree which possesses small tiny leaves on its shoot. it makes a great bonsai tree when well taken care and shaped.

Azalea

This bonsai tree possesses beautiful flowers which add to its beauty. it is a well-respected tree as far as bonsai is concerned.

Bahama berry bonsai tree.

some bonsai cultivators loves using the bahama berry for their bonsai cultivation. it adapts well when used as a bonsai tree with nice and pleasant odors radiating from the tree.

Bald cypress bonsai tree

The bald cypress bonsai tree is a popular deciduous tree used for bonsai. it has needle-like leaves which grows in rows of two along its slender wigs.

Chapter 4: Basics of Bonsai planting

How to choose a good bonsai

When choosing a Bonsai tree, there are several things to keep in mind. First and foremost among these is whether you plan to keep your Bonsai tree indoors, outdoors or both. There is no right or wrong way when it comes to where your tree is placed; it is a decision that will dictate, to some extent, how you care for you tree through the years.

The types of trees that do well indoors are Kingsville Boxwood, Ficus, Gardenia, and Serissa. Some types that like being outdoors better are Maple, Cedar, Elm, Beech, and Ginko.

If you're going to move your Bonsai tree back and forth between indoors and out, stick with a type of tree known for being hardy. Many trees in the Evergreen family are considered fine choices for indoor/outdoor growing. Your local environment is the most important factor when choosing where to grow your Bonsai.

It is also a good idea to take a look at the various species of trees and bushes that are commonly used for Bonsai cultivation and decide which type you'd like to try your hand at growing. Many common and familiar types of trees are perfectly adaptable to being Bonsai trees. Not all will be suitable to your local environment, though, so make sure you do a little research first.

Juniper is considered a good choice for many Bonsai hobbyists. This type of tree is a hardy evergreen (evergreens are a type of tree that never loses its leaves) and can survive and thrive in just about any local. It is perfectly suited to the varied climate conditions found throughout North America. It is also one of the easiest types of trees to train and cultivate. Juniper is very good at responding to the influence of the cultivator; it is easily convinced to hold just about any shape and is comfortable both indoors and out. For these reasons, it is the Juniper that is most often recommended to the beginner.

Aside from evergreens, conifers (cone-bearing, commonly needle bearing trees and bushes) and deciduous (leafy trees) families also offer many viable options. You may choose from dozens of varieties of pines, spruce, elms, oaks, Japanese Maple and many others.

Your Bonsai tree will always need access to sunlight, keep that in mind when you are choosing a spot for your tree. If you are going to grow it primarily indoors, placing it near a window will provide all the sunlight your tree could want. If you are going the outdoor route, pick a nice sunny spot so you won't have to re-position your tree too often.

How to prepare to grow a bonsai

Once you have decided on a type of Bonsai to grow and where you'll be keeping it and how large you'd like it to grow eventually, there is one more preliminary concern to address. When starting your Bonsai tree, there are three commonly acceptable ways from which to choose. The simplest way is to purchase a Bonsai tree that has already been cultivated for a few years and continue to care for it. The advantages of this method are obvious. It is simple and allows you to start right away without waiting for a seed to grow or a cutting to take root and establish itself. Cost can be a major drawback here. Bonsai trees can range in price from slightly under fifty dollars to around one thousand dollars, depending on the amount of care they have already received and the species being considered.

Growing a Bonsai from seed is another way to start your Bonsai tree. Be prepared to wait as long as half a decade for your tree to take shape. The good thing about this approach is that you will have near total control over every aspect of the trees growth process. It can be molded to your exact specifications, without compromise. This freedom from compromise comes at the cost of waiting several years to see your vision of your Bonsai tree begin to take shape. You can decide for yourself whether or not the wait is worth the extra degree of control.

Starting a Bonsai from a cutting is the perfect compromise between waiting a long while for your seed to sprout and buying a Bonsai that has already begun to be shaped. A cutting is just a piece of another tree that is planted in soil. It then begins to grow roots and will become a separate tree. This process cuts years off of waiting for a tree from seed and allows you to begin working with your tree almost right away, as you would be able to do with a purchased tree. When working with cuttings, there is considerable, but not total, control over the final product of the tree.

After you have decided on a type of tree that is both pleasing and suitable to your environment, whether you will be growing your Bonsai indoors, outdoors, or a combination of both, and made up your mind about how to obtain a tree, seeds or a cutting, there are some other factors to consider. You'll want to choose a pot for your Bonsai and decide on a style of growing it.

How to grow a bonsai from a seed

This is the most time-intensive and difficult way to start a Bonsai tree. Aside from the amount of time you have to wait before it is ready to train and prune, growing a tree requires much more time and effort than many are willing to give. If you want to try growing a Bonsai tree from seed, consider starting the tree as you would any other plant. Research the species of tree you want to grow and make sure you can meet its requirements. Your young tree will most likely be spending its formative years indoors, and this will require the ability to duplicate, it's natural environmental conditions. Depending on your location and the type of tree you are growing, you'll need to be able to control the internal temperature and lighting in addition to several other factors.

No Matter which method of starting your tree you choose, there are several things that need to be paid attention to no matter what. Each species of tree will require different standards of care and attention from you. Some of the most important contributing factors to the success of your Bonsai are:

Location

as previously stated, think ahead about whether you want to keep your tree inside or out. Traditionally in Japan Bonsai are grown indoors, but you shouldn't let tradition stop you.

Indoor Bonsai growing is both popular and necessary for those who live in less than ideal climates for outdoor growing.

Soil

Bonsai trees require a different kind of soil than most plants. A common soil mixture consists of thirty percent pumice and 70 percent what is known as "Akadama soil" This is a special type of clay based soil that is native to Japan. While it is possible to mix your own Bonsai soil, it is much easier to buy a readymade batch from a Bonsai dealer. A few minutes of internet research will turn up more than a few reputable supply houses.

Access to Sunlight

All trees and plants need copious amounts of sunlight. It is your job to provide your Bonsai tree with enough light. Usually, indoors, it is enough to place the tree near a sunny window. If you are unable to supply your Bonsai with natural sunlight, consider the use of a grow light.

Tools

There are many specialized tools that are meant to make caring for and pruning Bonsai trees as easy a process as possible. While it is nice to have specialized tools specifically for tending to Bonsai, they are often expensive and very similar to standard gardening tools. A nice pair of shears is recommended and a set of miniature basic gardening tools should suffice the beginner just fine.

How to select a healthy starter bonsai

The roots

Strong and healthy roots are key when considering a plant to use for Bonsai. Have a good look at a tree's base and roots to make sure it appears to have a strong foundation. It is best when the plants base appears to spread out gently in a radial pattern. The foundation should provide stability and also invite a viewers eyes up from the base to explore the rest of the tree. An unstable looking plant will make it harder to create a well-balanced, beautiful Bonsai.

The trunk

We are now slowly making up way up from the base of the tree to its midsection. The trunk is very important to examine and the qualities to look out for differ depending on the style of the plant. Usually, a thick, stable base which tapers gently as it increases in height will make for a suitable tree. If you are considering a formal upright style Bonsai, then it is important for the plant to have a very straight trunk. If you are thinking about going with other styles, then some curvature and other "moves" in the trunk are important to examine.

Branching pattern

Observing proper branching is a little more difficult to master. Most garden centers and nurseries do not have trained Bonsai plants, so you will have to do some research. If you notice a tree having thick lower branches and thinner higher ones, you may have found a suitable match. These would be the branches that form the main structure of your Bonsai. The plant should also only have small leaves. If the leaves are overly large, it will result in a Bonsai that looks out of proportion. At times it can be a little difficult to see the right fit and balance of branches with the tree's trunk. If you do not feel that you see the right branching pattern move on and keep searching. You will feel it when you have found the right tree to work with.

Health

A step that definitely cannot be skipped is examining the plant for good health. For your first couple of Bonsai plants it is better to skip on a plant you are not 100 percent confident in or sure of. If you are not convinced the tree is healthy then move on to the next one. It will need to be strong enough to handle your experimenting with wiring, pruning and potting.

For examining health I recommend that you remove the plant from its container. This way you can better check that everything is in good shape. Observe if there are any white fibrous roots (this is a positive sign for good health and growth) around its soil.

Aging potential

The final step to consider when picking out a tree is its potential for having an aged look. In Bonsai it is very important for a tree to look old. This aged look is primarily made possible by the tree's bark and trunk. The bark should have an attractive look and the trunk should have good girth. What also gives the appearance of more age is having some of the tree's root structure above soil. Having about 1/3rd of the tree's roots exposed will create a beautiful dramatic scene perfect for Bonsai.

How to choose the best pot for your bonsai

Japanese pottery is often the best pot to use for bonsai growing. These are high-quality pots, unglazed, natural and elegant but can be very expensive. Chinese pottery is often much cheaper compared to Japanese pottery. These generally are of lesser quality than Japanese ones but are currently improving to be considered as good pots or bonsai growing. Chinese pottery is commonly brightly glazed. An exception is Chinese antique pots. These antique pots are more expensive.

Old trees that have already been repotted for a number of times and already trained won't need frequent changes of pots compared to younger trees. Hence, more expensive pots can be used for these because they have already adapted well to life in small pots. For younger bonsai trees, repotting is more frequent, as the roots would need more room for growth. Training these would take a step-by-step process that involves a series of repotting. For this, it would be more economical to use plastic containers or less expensive pots.

Size

Size is another important consideration in choosing the right pot for bonsai trees. Trees that are still under training should be placed in larger containers. This will provide enough space for the roots to grow. Larger containers during the training period help the tree to cope better with the intensity of the training techniques applied to it, such as style-pruning. As the training progresses, the roots are gradually pruned until the tree has already adapted to growing in small pots. Once the trees have matured and are already trained, smaller pots can be used. The root systems should already be compact. At this point, aesthetic considerations are already among the prime reasons for bonsai pot choices.

Aesthetics

Aside from size, there are also other important considerations. These include shape, color and unglazed/glazed. To help with making the right choice, here are some guidelines. However, these are not hard and fast rules. Personal aesthetic choice will still play a larger role.

- Unglazed pots are commonly preferred among bonsai growers of pine trees and other conifers.

- Both unglazed and glazed bonsai pots can be used for deciduous trees. Experts recommend reserving the use of brightly glazed pots for trees that have flower and/or fruits.

- The width of the pot should approximately be equal to 2/3 of the bonsai tree's current height.

- How deep the pot is should be the same as the trunk base's thickness. However, this rule may be deferred when planting or repotting trees with very thin trunks or young bonsai trees.

Chapter 5: Basics for growing a bonsai

Basic tools you need for growing a bonsai

Bending and Protective Tools

In cases where you need to bend the trunk or branches of your bonsai heavily, you must take protective measures to avoid tearing the bark, breaking the wood, and to help with the healing of small fissures and cracks that may result from bending. Most people use wet raffia to tightly wrap around the area you plan to bend before applying the wire. You may also use bicycle tube or fusing rubber tape for the same purpose. For the parts of your plant where you plan to attach guy or fixation wires, you can protect them by wrapping them with infusion or fish tank hoses. For bending heavily, you can use ergonomically designed tools like rubber-padded steel levers and special screw clamps that come in different sizes and shapes. For bending sturdy trunks, iron rebars can be very useful too.

Electric Tools

When you think there is a need to use electric tools or power tools, make sure you know how to use these properly and safely. You need extreme caution when working with such tools in order to avoid injuries while working on your bonsai. Also, when working with electric tools, concentrate fully on the task and make sure you're alert and awake while you work. Although you may not need these tools as a beginner bonsai grower, it's still a good idea to be aware of what they are. Some of the basic examples of electric tools include:

angled carving hook, branch splitter, carving tools, curved scalpel, cut carving tools, gas torch, jin liquid, , protective glasses, round carving hook, small carving tools, small loop knife, spear plough, strong, straight scalpel, various circular brushes etc

Knives and Saws

You need these tools for cutting trunks, roots or branches of your bonsai which are either too hard or too thick for pliers or shears. You must also know how to use these properly, so you don't end up bending or breaking them. In order to smooth the wounds and cuts left by saws and pliers, you can use a grafting knife just like the professionals. Some basic examples of these tools are:

grafting knife, medium-sized or large foldable saw, sickle knife sickle saw, thin pruning saw.

Maintenance Tools

For when you need to remove dirt and rust that has accumulated on the blades of your tools, you can use rust erasers. For when you need to sharpen your blades, you may use grindstones which are available in different types. For maintaining blades and hinges, you may use camellia oil or gun oil. You may also want to have coco brushes on-hand to sweep up soil surfaces, trunks, tools, and more.

Repotting Tools and for Working on Roots

When you need to remove your bonsai's root ball, you need to use special sickle knives and sickle saws to cut along the pot's interior. For this task, solid angular bowls made of plastic make your work cleaner, more comfortable, and easier. Other tools for repotting and root work include root rakes and root hooks which come in different variants and sizes. When it comes to pruning roots, you can use a standard pair of strong shears with a solid handle and strong blades. There are also soil scoops available in varying sizes that you can use to scoop and pour soil. For removing weeds, applying moss, and performing other tasks, a tweezer spatula will come in handy.

Wiring Tools

When it comes to wiring bonsai, you need wire with different diameters, pliers to bend the wire, and a wire cutter. These are the basic tools needed which also come in various sizes and shapes. For the wire, the easiest to apply is aluminum, but copper works well too.

Watering Tools

The most basic tool for watering is a watering can which comes in all sizes and shapes. But for bonsai, it's best to choose one with a long neck and a fine nozzle. Other watering tools include a ball-shower for when you need to water a couple of trees. For a larger collection of bonsai trees, you may go with a garden hose with a built-in sprinkler stick. You may also need spray cans to spray your bonsai with plant products like fertilizers or to mist your plant once in a while. There are also watering systems available which water your bonsais automatically at a set time. Of course, these are more advisable for when you have many plants to care for.

Basic care tips for growing a healthy bonsai

Where to place your bonsai

No matter where you place your bonsai, it will surely bring a natural calming feel to your space. It will add an enchanting element to your home, office or even outdoors. Just be sure that the location of your bonsai allows it to bask in direct sunlight regularly, so it won't wither away.

For you to determine the best place to display your miniature tree, you should first know the type of plant you have and whether it's more suitable to grow outdoors or indoors. Outdoor bonsai thrive well when they get a lot of sunlight and when they are exposed to the changing of the seasons. Indoor bonsai thrive well in stable temperatures all year long.

Finding the right soil

When it comes to the soil for your bonsai, you must find a type of soil that can retain some water but also drains quickly. It must also contain tiny particles which help aerate the soil in order for the roots to gain access to oxygen. You can find specialty soils online or in your local gardening shop for your bonsai. Make sure to choose the right soil for your plant to survive and grow into a healthy tree.

Watering your bonsai

Although this is one of the most obvious things to do for your bonsai, watering bonsai isn't the same as watering other types of plants. There are specific requirements and steps to water your bonsai properly in order to maintain its health.

Pruning your bonsai

The main goal of pruning bonsai is to help maintain the shape you want your plant to have as it is growing. Pruning is also essential as it ensures the continuous growth of the bonsai tree. There are specific tools to use for pruning your bonsai to keep you from causing damage to any of its parts. Also, you should first think about what shape or style you want your bonsai to have, so you can prune it accordingly.

Repotting your bonsai

This is an important aspect of bonsai growing. The goal of repotting bonsai is for the removal of excess roots that may cause the bonsai's starvation. Also, repotting your bonsai ensures that it can keep growing in its small container. It's important to repot your bonsai at least one time every two years or so depending on the growth rate of your bonsai.

Styling and shaping techniques

Shaping the roots of your bonsai

The whole root system of a bonsai consists of the underground structure and the roots which are exposed on the surface. The latter are known as the "nebari." Cultivating healthy nebari is essential to the proper growth of your bonsai and to give it a true bonsai appearance. If you have decided to purchase an older plant as your first bonsai, there are special steps you must take in order to re-shape the nebari, especially if they haven't been maintained well in the past. In such a case, you may have to prune the sub-surface roots to ensure optimal growth. But if you start growing your bonsai from seed or you've purchased a starter plant, you can start working on the nebari sooner.

As aforementioned, you would have to repot your bonsai regularly as it grows. This is the perfect time for you to prune the nebari of your bonsai. But before you start pruning, you must first make sure that the nebari are spaced evenly, healthy, and they are growing well. Also, it's only recommended to prune the parts of the nebari that aren't necessary such as the outgrowths. Each time you repot your bonsai, prune the nebari in order to shape it well. Here are the methods to use when shaping the nebari.

Cutting

This involves cutting off the unnecessary and undesirable parts of the nebari including the phloem, bark, and cambium. However, be careful not to cut too deep that you would reach the root's structure. After cutting, leave your plant alone for some time to allow the roots to continue growing.

Air Layering

This also involves the removal of the phloem, bark, and cambium of your bonsai. But instead of leaving your plant alone after, air layering involves wrapping the open roots to retain their moisture. Most people use moistened sphagnum moss as wrapping. Over time, new roots start growing on the wrapped surface. This is an excellent method to promote the development of roots; however, it can be quite a challenge to maintain.

Grafting

For this method, you can perform it on its own or combine it with the other two methods. Grafting involves attaching a bonsai tree with the same species to a mature bonsai tree in the area where you want to promote the growth of roots. Over time, the younger plant will take root in the area.

Shaping the trunk of your bonsai

The term "kokejun" refers to the taper of the bonsai's trunk. Ideally, the trunk should have a thick base with even tapering towards the center and top. Since bonsai can't achieve this naturally, you have to guide and train your bonsai for it to grow this way. Growing bonsai requires an increase in the thickening of the trunk and tapering. You can do this by improving its "tachiagari"—the bonsai's initial growth and rise. And the best way to do this is by pruning carefully.

Also, you must consider the curves of your bonsai's trunk as well as the refinements of its form. Think about the form you want your bonsai to have so you can plan how to achieve it as your bonsai is growing. From the location of the branches to the distribution of foliage, leaf reduction and more, planning must start from the beginning while you still have a young tree with a pliable trunk. Here are the basic forms of bonsai which you may consider:

Bunjingi

This is also known as a bonsai's literati form and it's based on the definite line the tree forms. The foliage, limbs, and trunk of the bonsai would have to be trained to emphasize the line by following it. This form differs from the others in a very subtle way though it does have a very prominent trunk.

48

Chokkan

This is the most traditional form of bonsai and it's considered aesthetically natural because this is how trees usually look like in nature. Even if your bonsai has an organic form, you still need to pay attention to its growth and train it carefully as it is growing.

Moyohgi

This form is almost identical to chokkan but it's more informal. It has an upright form but it's not as symmetrical. For this, the trunk of the bonsai may be tilted slightly while still maintaining a basic vertical structure.

Chapter 6: How to choose the best soil for a bonsai

Tips for planting and soil

Making this choice is crucial to maintaining growth and proper development. The soil should have proper drainage suited for the tree species. It should not hold too much water, which can drown the tree or cause the roots to rot. It should not drain water too fast because it can wash away the nutrients, fertilizers, and the soil. It should be able to hold enough water long enough to allow the roots time to absorb moisture. Always check the soil mixture requirements of the bonsai tree species. Some species would need special soil mixes.

For most bonsai trees, a good soil mix is a ratio of ½ akadama to ¼ fine gravel and ¼ potting compost. If there won't be ample time to check and water the bonsai regularly, add more potting compost (has more water absorbing capacity) to retain moisture longer. If living in areas with a wet climate, add more akadama (with more draining characteristics) to promote less moisture retaining capacity. This will avoid soaking up the roots too much, which can lead to root rot or mushy roots.

Tips for repotting

Most bonsai will require repotting once per year to maintain their health.

Re-potting prevents bonsai from being pot-bound and encourages the growth of new feeder roots which let the tree absorb more moisture. The soil should be replaced with fresh soil at this time.

One way to know that it's time for repotting is when water takes a long time to drain or if you see roots looking like they are too crowded around the sides of your container.

Gently lift the tree out of its current container by tilting it to one side and moving it by the base of the trunk. If it is not coming free easily try gently tapping the container. If it still will not come free easily try gently poking a stick through the bottom to push the root ball out.

Then, carefully remove any other plants or decorations. A chopstick or knitting needle is helpful for this. Be gentle with any tangles in the roots. Begin on the edge and gradually work your way around. Try to "comb" the roots gently but don't pull or tug at them so as not to cause any damage to the main roots.

Continue to gently shake and brush off the soil until you have removed approximately half of the soil from the base and edge of your root ball.

Spray the roots with a little bit of water. This will help remove the old soil and will keep them from drying out while you are pruning them.

You will need very sharp scissors or bonsai cutters to prune the roots. Make sure you have rinsed away most of the soil first. If you cut through soil your scissors will get dull very quickly.

First, cut off any old brown roots that have grown close to the edge of the container. These restrict the growth of new feeder roots and should be removed. Cut off at least a third to a half of these old roots. Be careful not to cut any new feeder roots.

Then, begin cutting the thinner roots that hang below the depth of your container. Trim them into a shape that is suitable for your container and that will leave a space of about a half inch to ¾ inch between the roots and the edge of your container.

Wash out the container or choose a new pot that suits your tree. Cover the drain holes with wire mesh. The tree will need something to anchor it so that it doesn't get blown over by the wind or tip over from being moved.

Thread some wire through the drain holes to create an anchor. Then pour in a thin layer of gravel. Top it off with a layer of fresh new soil.

Decide where you will position your tree in the pot. Likely somewhere slightly off center and towards the back. Make a small mound of soil where you are going to place your bonsai. Gently place your plant on the mound and spread its roots evenly across the soil.

When you are satisfied with the position of your tree, take the wires that you threaded though the drain holes and twist them together over the root ball until it is held firmly enough not to tip from the wind. Do not make it so tight that you damage the roots. These wires must be left in place for a few months until your tree roots settle in.

Chapter 7: How to properly prune your bonsai

Bonsai plants and fertilizers

Fertilizing is adding more plant food to support growth. This is very important during the growth season to maximize growth potential. Adding fertilizers at the right time supports strong, sturdy trunks, healthy branches, and bright foliage. Bonsai roots have a limited area to expand and search for food. Whatever nutrients present in the soil can be quickly used up. To keep the bonsai adequately nourished, adding fertilizers is vital.

Basic Fertilizer Components

Fertilizers contain the 3 basic compounds nitrogen (N), potassium (K) and phosphorus (P). Each of these elements serves specific purposes in plant growth. Nitrogen supports the growth of the stems and leaves. Potassium supports the growth and development of flowers and fruits. Phosphorus supports the healthy growth of the root system.

Fertilizers come in various ratios of these elements. And each ratio is used at certain times of the year, depending on season and stage of growth.

When to fertilize

The best time to fertilize is during the bonsai tree's growth season. Apply the right ration during the entire growth period, which is usually from early spring until the middle of autumn. Bonsai trees grown indoors can be fertilized throughout the year.

Fertilizing may do more harm than good in some instances. When a bonsai tree is repotted, most experts agree not to fertilize for a month. Allow the roots to establish themselves well first in the new environment before giving them any fertilizers. Also, when a tree is sick, postpone the application of fertilizers. The concentration may be too much for the tree to handle and worsen the condition.

How to choose the right fertilizer

To maximize growth, the right kind of fertilizer should be used at the right time. During the early spring, the best fertilizer to use on bonsai trees would be one that has a relatively high concentration of nitrogen, such as NPK 12:6:6. This is best for boosting bonsai tree growth. In the summer season, the best fertilizer is one with a balanced ratio of NPK, such as NPK 10:10:10. In the autumn, the fertilizer should help harden the bonsai for the winter season. An example is NPK 3:10:10.

Aside from growth, different types of fertilizers are also given to the bonsai trees to promote certain traits or support certain plant development. For example, a fertilizer like NPK 6:6:12 applied to bonsai trees encourages flowering. Older bonsai trees would thrive better with fertilizers that have lower nitrogen concentrations. Or, just use the same ratio but in fewer quantities.

Fertilizers are basically the same. Regular fertilizers used for gardening can be used safely on bonsai trees. Just make sure that the ratio used is right for the season and the tree growth stage. Solid or liquid fertilizers are totally fine. It's best to use fertilizer covers when choosing to use solid fertilizers. These covers will help keep the fertilizer in place and be used by the plant. Follow closely the application guidelines on the packaging of the chosen fertilizer.

When applying fertilizers, follow the recommendations on the packaging. However, reduce the amounts slightly when applying fertilizers to bonsai trees that are no longer being trained. Fertilizing at this point is for balancing growth and not for stimulating it. Avoid applying too much fertilizer and stick to the directions for use. Overfeeding does more harm than good. Giving too much fertilizer will not make the bonsai tree grow faster or bigger over a shorter period. Sometimes, it will cause stunted growth, wilting, and even death.

Pests, infections and disease remedies

The first step in curbing pests and diseases is to monitor the bonsai tree regularly. If you start to have this problem, it is best to catch it as soon as possible. There are ways that would give you an indication that something is wrong with the tree if you happen to not notice issues upon inspection.

First of these signs being the leaves. If you notice that the leaves are wilting or turning brown or yellow, this is a big indication. Also, the leaves could start being covered in spots, holes or fall off the tree altogether. As a note, the leaves can have these same issues even without diseases or pests being present. Look for changes in the environment or maintenance routine to get to the root of the problem.

Other signs that your tree might be subject to pests is that the tree is not growing as fast as usual or there may be creamed colored larvae in the soil or on the tree itself. More evidence of pests is that there is a sticky residue left on the tree. The more obvious is when red spider mites attack your bonsai when you see webbing in between the leaves or branches. This pest is especially important to look for when the bonsai is a juniper.

If you find that your bonsai tree is infected, this is where you take a closer work. This is where it can get tricky, especially if the infection is in the roots. Once you have pinpointed the culprit, there are a few methods that generally can be followed to treat the bonsai tree from the infection or infestation.

1. Any leaves that have become diseased or infected should be removed to ensure it does not spread to other areas of the bonsai.

2. In the case of the leaves that have fallen off of an infected or infested tree, dispose of them carefully so that they will not continue to spread.

3. The tree should be relocated to a place that is secluded from any other plants to make sure the infestation or infection spreads to other plants.

4. A fungicide that is specific to the cause should be used as per the instructions.

5. If present, pests, and insects can be removed by hand picking them off of the tree or spraying with a water hose.

6. If the bonsai tree is located outside, another alternative may be to introduce healthy ladybugs which will eat most insects.

7. A mild solution of soap and water or a specific insect soap can be used to wash the pests away from the tree.

8. Any remaining insects and pests can be treated with an insecticide particular to the infestation. This can be sprayed directly onto the leaves or combined with the soil.

9. All tools used for the bonsai that has become infected or infested need to be thoroughly sterilized. This can be done with rubbing alcohol or disinfectant.

10. If a fungal infection is present, the soil should be removed and discarded away from the property. It is not to be used again by any other plant for fear of the infection continuing to live in the soil.

11. If you decide to use the container again, it needs to be scrubbed and washed thoroughly before being used again.

12. The bonsai tree should be moved to a place which has good ventilation.

Treatment of Specific Pests and Insects

Red Mites

These very small insects can lead to the death of your bonsai. They are usually located on the bottom of the leaves and can easily be missed unless closely inspected. Sometimes evidence of their presence can be seen when there is a very fine web located on the foliage.

One foolproof way of checking is to just a white sheet of paper. Hold the paper underneath a branch as you lightly tap the branch. If the red mites are present, they will fall on the paper, making them more noticeable. The recommended treatment is to use an organic insect soap or insecticide and apply directly to the underside of the foliage.

Scale Insects

These are also a very small pest which is brown, white or yellow. They create a sticky substance which may be the first sign that you notice that your bonsai has been infested. Otherwise, this is a difficult insect to spot as they are usually located under the bark. Owners of Fukien Tea Bonsais need to monitor their tree for this type of pest.

The recommended treatment is to use your hands to remove the insects. Scales have a protective shell which is difficult to infiltrate making insecticides less effective as a sure treatment of their infestation. Also, because they are located under the bark, it is best when they move to other sections of the bonsai to pick them off the tree.

Vine Weevils

These pests are able to be seen easily when the adults lay their eggs into the soil. Like most pests, these weevils can create a lot of damage to your bonsai trees. When the eggs hatch, the larvae will attack and eat the roots of the tree, going undetected. One way of knowing there is a problem is that the leaves will start to wilt.

The recommended treatment is to use an insecticide to remove the adult insects so they can be prevented from laying more eggs. Then the plant will need to be re-potted in a new container and soil. As the tree is being transplanted, remove all larvae present to prevent an infestation from occurring again. As an added measure, the insecticide can be combined with the new soil.

Caterpillars

This pest is much easier to notice because of their size. Also because they will leave obvious holes in the foliage of the bonsai tree. They are able to cause a decent amount of damage in a short period, especially if there are several.

The best treatment that is recommended is to remove the caterpillars by hand. To ensure they all have been removed, you can couple insect spray with the treatment.

Mealy Bugs

Being a silent pest, they can start to feed on the root system in addition to being under the branches and leaves themselves. They have white balls like cotton in which they hide in clusters. The best-recommended treatment is to use contact insecticide or use a systematic spray.

Slugs and Snails

These pests are dormant except when the temperature is 50° Fahrenheit (10° Celsius) during the spring months. They are able to be noticed because of their size or by the slimy trails they secrete. The treatment that is recommended is to take them off the tree by hand. If the bonsai is located outdoors, the use of slug bait can be an effective way to ensure they will infest the tree again.

Treatment of Specific Diseases and Infections

Root Rot

This is a common issue which occurs when there is too much moisture retained in the soil. This happens usually when a heavy soil such as peat is being used, the plant is being watered too often or there are not enough drainage holes in the container. The longer this condition remains, the more chance there is that the roots will start to deteriorate. This affects the entire tree as it starts to lose nutrients and the foliage will probably turn brown. You may also press against the trunk and it feels soft. If not treated, the entire bonsai will die. In the case of under watering, this can occur in a matter of days. It takes a few weeks for the roots to rot if you have been overwatering your bonsai.

The best treatment is removing the roots that are affected by pruning them away from the good roots. Then transplant the tree into another container with proper drainage holes. Use soil which drains well. Follow the watering recommendations found in chapter seven about proper hydration of your bonsai tree to prevent this from happening again. Discard the soil as it may still have the infection present.

Rust

This is an infection that will be noticed on the underside of the foliage. It appears as a small raised section which can be a range of colors between brown, red, orange or yellow. Another indication is that the leaves will start to curl and then fall off of the bonsai tree. The best way to control this infection is to prune the affected leaves before they spread further.

Leaf Spot

This is a type of fungal infection which has stages. The first thing that will be observed is there will be white spots which appear on the foliage. During the next stage of the infection, the color of the spot's changes to gray, brown or black. In the final stages of infection, the affected leaves will fall off the tree. The treatment is to remove the infected leaves off of the tree and then apply a spray fungicide over the entire tree.

Black Spot

This is a virus which affects the foliage of the bonsai trees, especially the Chinese Elm. The result of this virus is that the leaves turn yellow and then they fall off of the tree. The recommended treatment is to prune the infected leaves and then treat the complete tree with a spray fungicide.

Mildew

When the tree is located in damp conditions, this fungus will probably thrive. White powder will be noticeable and present on the foliage and cannot be removed simply by brushing the powder off the leaves. The treatment which is recommended is the leaves which are affected the need to be removed. The remaining foliage needs to be washed with water and soap as this fungus spreads by spores. This process may need to be repeated multiple times until the fungus has been completely removed.

Twig and Tip Blight

This disease occurs during warm weather and when the soil has retained too much moisture. The result of this disease is that the tips of the bonsai leaves will turn brown and then fall off of the tree. The recommended treatment is to remove the leaves that are affected and then use a disinfectant where the foliage was pruned to keep the disease from infecting other areas.

Chapter 8: Wiring techniques and clamping

Wiring and clamping are techniques used in bonsai training. Wiring gives you control over the growth of your bonsai. You would use wires to shape the branches and trunk of your tree, so they will grow to the shape you desire. As soon as your bonsai has an established root system, you can begin this process. Wiring isn't a one-time thing—it's a continuous process that you would have to do stage by stage depending on how you want your bonsai to grow into maturity.

Wiring is essential for shaping your bonsai because these miniature trees don't grow into the forms we desire naturally. Through the process of wiring, you can guide the growth of the tree allowing it to grow in unnatural—but visually appealing—forms. To simply put it, wiring is done to contribute to the aesthetics of a bonsai tree. Through wiring, you can form your bonsai artistically to show off your own style and personality.

The types of wire used for bonsai wiring are either aluminum or copper wire. For this task, choose a wire that is approximately a third of the trunk's or branch's diameter. Aluminum wire is recommended for beginners because it's easier to manipulate. It's more flexible than copper, but it's not as sturdy. If you decide to use aluminum wire, you must monitor the trunk or branches that you have wired every two weeks. On the other hand, copper wire is sturdier and harder. This means that it's able to hold its form for a longer time without getting detached or displaced. However, copper wire may end up causing damage to your bonsai's trunk or branches if you don't monitor it carefully. When left unchecked and unattended, this type of wire might cut or bruise parts of your plant. Therefore, you must monitor the condition and growth of your bonsai regularly after wiring.

To achieve the form, you desire for your bonsai, it's best to start wiring while your plant is young and healthy. The best time to start wiring is after repotting as this will help support the new growth. The perfect time for wiring also depends on the type of bonsai you're growing. For instance, proper timing differs between deciduous and coniferous trees:

- The best time to wire deciduous trees is during the early part of the spring season. Do this when new buds are starting to develop on your bonsai's limbs. This is the perfect time for wiring as it provides an ideal appearance of the branches and trunk of your bonsai before new growth and leaves start developing. This means that you can clearly see the limbs which, in turn, allows you to apply the wire without distractions.

- The best time to wire coniferous trees is between late autumn and early winter. The reason for this is that the foliage of these types of bonsai trees renew every year. This means that the limbs will always have foliage no matter the time of the year. You can start wiring when the sap is at the lowest part of the branches. This makes them more flexible and easier to wire.

One thing to remember is that you shouldn't wire your bonsai if it's suffering from a disease or any other kind of condition. Also, check the strength of the branches before wiring as weak branches might break when you apply wire to them. Make sure your plant is strong and healthy first, especially the parts you plan to wire. That way, you won't end up damaging your tree in the process.

Various techniques to try

Wiring is a process that's crucial for bonsai training and styling. This involves wrapping wire around the trunk or branches of your miniature tree. This allows you to bend, reposition, and style your bonsai to achieve the final form you want it to have when it matures. Wiring isn't an easy or fast process. In fact, it may take a couple of months before the wired parts of your bonsai will be permanently set. Only then can you remove the wire carefully.

There are a lot of things involved in wiring—it's a very tricky process to learn. The two main wiring techniques are double-wiring which involves wiring two branches adjacent to each other and having the same thickness to each other and single-wiring which involves wiring branches one at a time. Wire all of the branches that you want to shape before you start bending them. Start wiring branches from the trunk of your bonsai to the main branches, then the tree's secondary branches. Make sure that the wire you use is thick enough to support the trunk or branches you want to bend and shape. Now, let's go through these main wiring techniques step by step:

Double-wiring

- Choose two branches adjacent to each other and with the same thickness.

- Make an estimation of the length of wire you need for the task.

- Before wiring these branches, wrap the wire around your bonsai's trunk twice so it doesn't move around.

- Continue by wiring the base of the first branch all the way to the tip. Then you can start wiring the second branch.

- Make sure to wrap the wire at a 45-degree angle as this allows the wire to promote the thickening of the tree while it follows the new shape.

Single-wiring

- Make an estimation of the length of wire you need for the task.

- Wrap the wire around the trunk twice first before you start wiring branches one at a time at a 45-degree angle.

- If you plan to wire several branches in one area, make sure to arrange the wires neatly.

After wrapping the trunk and branches with wire, it's time to start bending them. Be careful when bending and repositioning so you don't break or damage the trunk or any of the branches of your bonsai. Gently grip the outer part of the branch and bend from the inside. This method ensures that you won't split or break the branches. Bending should be done in a singular motion—repeated bending may damage the branches. Also, you may want to step back after bending each of the branches to check the overall look of your bonsai to ensure that you're getting the look you planned to achieve.

Wire Anchoring

When wiring branches, you would have to wrap the wire at a certain angle—usually 45-degrees—around the branches. Before this, you should secure the wire first, so it doesn't move around when you start bending the branches. This is very important because when the wire starts twisting around as you bend your bonsai's branches, this causes damage, especially to the bark. The process of wire anchoring can help prevent this. There are different methods of wire anchoring you can do depending on the part of the bonsai:

Wire anchoring for the trunk

When wiring the trunk of your bonsai, you can anchor the wire into its growing medium. To do this, insert a significant length of the wire into the soil. Make sure that the anchored wire is adjacent to the trunk, it's coiled around the trunk twice, and there aren't any gaps.

Wire anchoring for the branches

When wiring the branches of your bonsai, anchor the wire by wrapping it around the trunk at least two times.

Wire anchoring for branch forks

Loop the wire over the branch forks first before you start wrapping the wire around the branches. Position the loop over the branch fork if you plan to bend the branches upward. Position the loop below the branch fork if you plan to bend the branches downward.

Gaps and Spacing

Wiring is a process that involves both hands. You should hold the branches gently but firmly with one hand while using your other hand to apply the wire. Make sure that the wire you wrap around the branches is firmly pressed and in full contact with them. Otherwise, you will end up with gaps.

Basically, gaps are the areas where the wire isn't in contact with the trunk or branches. Gaps shouldn't exist for one very important reason. When it's time to start bending the branches and there are some branches which you need to "overbend" in order to get the form or position you desire, having gaps increases the risk of the branch breaking or snapping.

What does clamping mean

Clamping is another bonsai training technique, though it's not as common as wiring. You would perform clamping as part of shaping and styling your bonsai. Much like wiring, you may use clamping to change the growing direction of your bonsai's trunk or branches. Just make sure that when you perform this technique, you do it carefully and correctly so that the clamp won't damage your tree or create an unintended effect.

It's important to note that changing the growing direction of a bonsai's trunk or branches isn't required. But if you see your bonsai as a piece of art, then clamping can be a fun activity for you. After you have attached the clamp to your bonsai, leave it in position for some time. Over time, you can start tightening the clamp bit by bit in order to force the trunk or branches to grow in a certain direction. You may also move the position of the clamp to promote continuous growth in the right direction.

When it comes to clamping, one thing you shouldn't forget is that you should never make forceful movements with the tool. Instead, simply apply gentle pressure on your tree. This ensures that the circulation of your bonsai doesn't get cut off which, in turn, might end up killing your tree. If this is your first time to perform clamping, use the lightest setting first. Then as soon as you see some movement or a change in direction, you can start tightening the clamp little by little.

As with wiring, clamping is a slow process that requires patience and careful observation. Combining clamping and wiring allows you to change the growing direction of your bonsai's trunk and its branches too. But you only have to do this if you want to see a huge change in how your bonsai is growing. The length of time you would keep the clamp on your bonsai depends on how much of a change you want to make. There are some cases where people leave the clamps in place for a number of years!

Also, the type of clamp to use depends on the type of bend you want your bonsai to acquire. Even though all clamps possess bumper ends as a safety feature to not cause damage, there are several shapes and sizes available. This variation allows you to work on your bonsai tree no matter what size it is. Some clamps are even designed to be used alongside wiring techniques. You can also use clamps to straighten the trunk or branches of your bonsai. At the end of the day, it all depends on what you're trying to achieve through clamping.

Chapter 9: How to defoliate a bonsai tree

Most beginners deal with the same issue—being able to maintain the health of their bonsai. This is especially true for those who don't educate themselves enough before they start the process. For a lot of people, they believe that growing a bonsai is basically the same as growing any other kinds of plants. Of course, this isn't true. If you want to maintain a healthy bonsai, you should know how to take care of it properly.

Adding the aesthetic value of your tree involves allowing it to grow in a small, proportionate container with the appropriate type of soil. Growing and cultivating bonsai requires a lot of care and a broad knowledge of the different methods and techniques used specifically for bonsai. In this article, we will be focusing on defoliation and deadwood techniques which are also an important part of the whole process.

Defoliation is a crucial process though not all types of plants can adopt it. Nevertheless, defoliation allows the dwarfing of foliage to some types of deciduous trees. On the other hand, deadwood techniques are typically applied to the branches of coniferous trees. While deciduous trees shed their branches regularly and the wounds left are able to heal after some time, coniferous trees retain their dead limbs. After some time, these limbs start getting eroded and weathered. You may remove these limbs completely or partially though this might end up causing damage to your tree's shape or its aged appearance. If you want to retain these limbs, you must treat them chemically for their preservation and give them the proper coloration. Also, you need to shape the deadwood so that it fits into your aesthetic plan.

How to Defoliate Your Bonsai Plant

Defoliating bonsai is a process wherein you cut all of the leaves when the summer season comes along. This process forces your bonsai to grow new leaves; therefore, increasing ramification and decreasing the leaf size. You should only perform defoliation if you're growing a deciduous type of bonsai tree. Also, you should only perform it if you know that your tree is healthy enough to survive defoliation—a very demanding process. When it comes to defoliation, you don't have to do this on the entire tree. You may only defoliate parts of it for the purpose of restoring balance in your bonsai.

Defoliation is an important technique for the aesthetic growth of your bonsai. It promotes the goal of growing bonsai—to create aesthetic pleasure, balance, and harmony. The main purpose of defoliation is the reduction of the size of your bonsai's leaves. Over time, this process may increase the number of leaves and stimulate growth as well. Another benefit of defoliation is that it can help stimulate the development of branchlets which, in turn, allows double the growth in one growing season.

If you have a deciduous type of bonsai tree, then you may consider defoliating it. But before you do, make sure that your tree is growing vigorously and is at the peak of health. The leaves of plants—including bonsai—help them grow. Photosynthesis happens in the leaves; therefore, if you start removing the leaves of a sick or an infected bonsai, this will make the condition worse. Although defoliation can be beneficial to your bonsai, it poses two major risks as well. First, it will shock your bonsai's system. Second, it will restrict your bonsai's ability to grow. So, if you have an unhealthy tree, defoliation might end up killing it.

Observe all aspects of your bonsai before making the decision to defoliate. If you see any weak branches, it's best to delay this process as it might weaken those branches further. Give them time to grow leaves, buds, and grow stronger too. If this is your first time to defoliate your bonsai, you should only defoliate a third of the whole tree until you gain more confidence and experience.

Although you may pinch off some buds and leaves using your fingers, the best type of tool for defoliation is a sharp pair of pruning scissors. This ensures that you can make clean cuts which will heal quickly and properly. To ensure the cleanliness of your pruning scissors, make sure to wipe them clean before and after each defoliation session. This also prevents the transmission of bacteria to the cuts and wounds.

The best month to perform defoliation is June. This gives ample time to your bonsai for growing new leaves in preparation for winter. Also, it's best to start defoliation after the new growths that emerged during the spring season has already hardened off. It's never a good idea to defoliate your bonsai when it's dormant. Instead, do this during the season when your bonsai is growing leaves actively. Here are the types of defoliation you can perform on bonsais:

Partial

This type of defoliation won't cause as much of a shock to your bonsai's system compared to complete defoliation. One reason for this is that the trauma felt by the bonsai gets spread out over the whole growing season. Another reason is that you would only remove a portion of the leaves. This means that a lot of smaller leaves will remain—and these will continue performing photosynthesis. Here are the steps to follow for partial defoliation:

- First, remove the biggest leaves—these typically grow at the tips of the branches. Removing these leaves gives space for light to pass through your bonsai to the lower and center parts thus stimulating vigorous growth.

- Continue defoliating by removing the rest of the large leaves. Over time, these will be replaced by smaller leaves.

It's as simple as that! After you've partially defoliated your bonsai, place it somewhere with a lot of sun. Also, give your bonsai a lot of water for it to recover faster. This type of defoliation is recommended for beginner bonsai growers. This is because there's a very low likelihood that you will make a mistake that would adversely affect the health and shape of your bonsai.

Complete

You may only attempt complete defoliation after you've gained more experience with partial defoliation. As the name suggests, this involves removing all the leaves of your bonsai. Only do this after the new leaves have completely hardened off—this means that they have a dark green color and they have already become tough and shiny. Here are the steps to follow for partial defoliation:

- Remove each of the leaves at their base while making sure that you've left the petioles (stems). As new buds emerge, these petioles will dry up and start falling off.

- Continue doing this until you've removed all the leaves of your bonsai. Once all of the leaves have been removed, it becomes easier for you to see your bonsai's overall structure.

After this process, place your bonsai in a place where it can get some—but not a lot—of sun. Also, your bonsai won't need a lot of water because there won't be any leaves left to feed. After a few weeks, new buds will start emerging. The leaves that grow from these buds will be significantly smaller since they would have less time to develop during the growing season.

Deadwood techniques for bonsai

Deadwood techniques for bonsai are performed for aesthetic and practical purposes. Dead wood can appear on bonsai which have encountered disease. As a bonsai grower, you have the choice to allow this dead wood to stay on your tree or you can remove it too. But as aforementioned, the removal of dead wood might cause harm to the aged illusion you want your bonsai to have. Doing this might also compromise the overall shape of your bonsai. This is actually why most bonsai growers leave dead wood alone. If you're one such person, you must have the dead wood on your bonsai treated. This ensures the preservation of the coloration of the dead wood. It's also important for you to do everything you can to prevent pests from harming your plant. Then, you should also shape the dead wood to fit into your aesthetic plans for your tree.

Deadwood techniques are essential, especially in terms of aesthetics. Seasoned bonsai growers know how to perform these techniques. But even as a beginner, you can learn these techniques to prepare yourself for when you need to start doing them on your own. Here are some benefits of performing deadwood techniques:

- To conceal the defects of your bonsai such as oversized parts or misplaced branches.

- It helps give your bonsai an illusion of being old.

- To disguise your bonsai's trunk after you have reduced it because it has grown excessively.

- To highlight the overall appearance of your bonsai.

Different deadwood techniques can be applied to different plants. To help you understand these techniques better, here are some things you should know:

Driftwood and Shari

The driftwood style applies to bonsais that have a large dead trunk holding dead branches. This style is also known as "sharamiki." You can carve the dead wood of the bonsai according to the shape that you want. In the end, it should look like the remains of a tree beaten by the weather.

Shari are usually found on a bonsai's main trunk. A small shari runs vertically or near the front of the trunk. Shari aren't very common because bonsai enthusiasts don't see them as having a lot of aesthetic value. Usually, living bark surrounds shari or it can be concealed by growing branches. The main factors that cause the formation of shari are lightning damage, failing branches or trunk damage.

Jin

This deadwood technique can be used on the branches of your bonsai. You can also use it at the top of your plant. The aim of the jin technique is to show your bonsai's age as well as its ability to survive the struggle over time. For this technique, you would have to completely remove the bark of the branch from a certain starting point. After doing this, the remaining wood starts to die, and this forms the jin.

Creating a jin at the top of your bonsai gives you a result that's highly visible. The reason for this is that the tapered bonsai goes through a proportion change that has a significant effect on the illusion of age. This technique allows you to remove branches that you don't want to be part of your bonsai. This helps increase the age illusion as it creates a shape that is bent over. The illusion you create will look like a branch near your bonsai's trunk that has been broken.

Takuni

This is one of the more interesting techniques as you would use a piece of deadwood to for creating a composite style of driftwood. This technique gives your bonsai a weathered appearance. With it, you can also use the lower part of your bonsai. For this, you would carve a channel or a groove into the trunk then place living material. Young juniper trees are ideal for this technique because they are flexible and they're able to withstand severe shaping. For this technique, you would make use of wire wrappings, screws, and even nails. Once these are placed firmly, you can continue cultivating the tree.

Chapter 10: Indoor and outdoor bonsai plants differences

How to grow an indoor bonsai plant

Temperature

Tree species which are tropical generally require temperatures that are high regularly, like that average room temperature of your house. Bonsai subtropical trees survive lower temperatures to some extent and when they escalate a season of winter, they flourish when temperatures are beneath normal temperature of a living room.

Amid the chilly months, when your bonsai is inside, the best prescription is setting it in a shallow plate loaded up with a layer of rock with water included. This gives additional dampness around the tree as the water dissipates and diminishes the measure of dampness lost to present day warming frameworks.

Watering and treating

The most essential guideline is; never water unnecessarily on a daily schedule since its indoor. Overlook the mark joined to your Bonsai tree which states you have to water each for days. Rather, screen your tree and possibly water when required. If you don't mind read the watering and preparing pages for progressively point by point data.

How to grow an outdoor bonsai plant

Watering

The timetable/schedule for your watering your bonsai tree plant may fluctuate or better still may be influenced with the size of the pot used, the kind of soil and the sort of bonsai tree you claim.

The watering of your bonsai should never be ignored. Apply water when the dirt seems dry - never enable the dirt to end up totally dry. On the off chance that your bonsai is getting full sun, it might be important to water once every day.

Assess each tree's water prerequisites and change your watering timetable to oblige it. It is a smart thought to utilize a dampness meter until you become acquainted with the prerequisites of your bonsai tree. Watering ought to be finished with a watering Can or Hose connection which ought to administer the water in a sufficiently delicate way as not to irritate the dirt. Water ought to be connected until it starts coming up short on the openings in the base of your pot. A decent downpour is normally an adequate watering.

You should think; how regularly would it be a good idea for you to water bonsai trees or how to deal with a bonsai tree? Dealing with a bonsai is so natural as long as you most likely are aware how to regard it as our guide on basic bonsai care as beneath.

87

As a matter of first importance, your bonsai needs water to flourish. At whatever point the dirt shows up or feels dry it's past time to water. Try not to enable your bonsai's dirt to dry out and at whatever point conceivable attempt to water in any event day by day (particularly if in direct daylight). All things considered, obviously, the size and area of your bonsai and the pruned holder it calls home will assume major job in how regularly you're topping her off.

Temperature

If all else fails, do as Mother Nature proposed, expose it to direct sunlight. In spite of their smaller than expected scale and imaginative excellence, bonsai trees are pretty much equivalent to they're colossal cousins. They have comparative necessities for daylight and temperature to flourish so the best wager on situating your developing tree is to discover what others of the species need. Ensure your indoor plants end up around southern confronting windows and the open air ones appreciate enough early morning beams with some evening shade. This is pretty much perfect for your bonsai.

Chapter 11: Bonsai seasonal care tips

How to take care of your bonsai during spring, summer, autumns and winter

Spring

Spring is the season of new beginnings. This is the perfect time to start new Bonsai, prune old ones and continue sharpening your skills. It is a great time to continue training your Bonsai and then let it grow and recover.

Summer

In the summer, Bonsai from forest trees should always be outside. They need sunny days, cool nights and great ventilation. If you want to bring one inside for viewing/displaying it can only be for 3 hours maximum.

If you live in an area that does not provide this type of summer climate you must try to recreate it. They need around 4 hours of direct sunlight every day, and then should be in the shade in the afternoon. Some enthusiasts also place their Bonsai on a slightly tilted stand. This way when it rains water can drain out of its pot more easily. Extreme conditions are never good for a Bonsai. Too much rain, sun, and wind will put your tree at risk.

Autumns

During autumn, it is time to prepare your Bonsai for winter. This is best done by slowing down its growth. Water the tree less frequently and do not fertilize it. I also recommend you to not prune or cut any branches after around the middle of August.

Winter

Winter is the riskiest time for a Bonsai. The consistent low temperatures and dry winds can easily kill a miniature tree. I recommend for you to protect your Bonsai when the temperature drops below 28 degrees Fahrenheit. That means placing it in a greenhouse, cold frame, or pit. These are all ways to protect your tree from frost.

If you opt for a cold frame, don't forget to water it while it is in there. Remember to carefully assess how much water it needs. It may only be necessary every other day.

Bonsai can generally still remain outside in temperatures above 15 °F as long as they have some protection. If temperatures drop below this, it may be necessary to bring them inside. This fluctuation of environmental change is actually also not good for the tree but it may be your only option in extreme situations. Woody plants must go through a period of cold dormancy. Without this they die.

Chapter 12: Common mistakes to avoid when growing bonsai trees and how to avoid them

Proper Watering

The biggest mistake that is made with new bonsai owners is that they do not properly water their tree. People will treat their bonsai like any other plant and water it accordingly. However, bonsai trees are particular about the watering schedule. It is possible to under or over water the tree, and there are many consequences that can arise when the moisture in the soil is not the correct balance. If the roots have not completely dried out, they are able to be saved by following the proper watering guidelines for your type of bonsai.

The role of water is important for any plant or tree. This is due to the leaves using nutrients and water to convert the energy from the sunshine and through the process of photosynthesis to create the sugars required to grow. Over 55% of the weight of the bonsai is water, and it aids in the nutrients being transported to the entire tree. The majority of this water is taken in by the root system. This is why watering and keeping the roots from rotting are the number one way to keep your bonsai thriving.

The way to determine the amount of water required is to first look at the type of soil that is being used. As a rule of thumb, most bonsais need to be watered when the soil becomes dry slightly. You do not want the soil to dry out or be waterlogged. Both of these instances will result in root rot. This is an important step because if it is not followed, it is possible to damage a bonsai beyond repair within a week's time.

Proper Soil

If you purchased a cheap Chinese bonsai, it likely came with clay-based soil. This is not ideal for the bonsai as most of the water will not be absorbed into the dirt but rather rest on the base of the container or has drained out of the pot. If your bonsai is in clay, transfer as soon as possible with soil suited for your variation of bonsai tree. Usually, this is a loose and gravel combination.

Bonsais do not grow well in potting soil and it should be avoided. There are specific blends available for bonsais which usually contain small particles which allow for the aeration of the soil as the roots require oxygen to function properly.

Fertilization is a key component for the soil. It needs to be combined with the soil during the growing season starting in the early spring months through the middle of the fall. The need for fertilization is required because of the nature of the shallow pots that bonsais are commonly planted. The roots are able to stretch out which searching for more nutrients during the growing season. However, they are not able to stretch far because of the limited space. This is why you need to replenish the nutrients in the soil as your bonsai grows.

Wrong Size Container

When you first purchase a bonsai, the size of the plant is also an important aspect that needs great care and attention. You cannot just select any pot for your bonsai as they need to be the correct shape and size and even color for your particular bonsai tree. The first aspect of container selection is to consider the root system. The pot needs to be large enough for the roots to be able to stretch slightly so it has space to grow until it is time to transplant. This also gives the roots the room they require gathering the nutrients and water from the soil.

Another aspect of container selection is the size of your bonsai and the root system. Do you want to keep the bonsai at the current size or do you want it to continue to grow? Is your tree more mature and grown to the size you wish it to be? If so, you would transfer it to another pot of similar size and shape as you are going to be pruning the root system each time it is re-potted. If you want it to still grow in size, place it in a slightly larger pot according to the desired final result. The perfect sized pot is one which is slightly smaller in width than the longest branches.

Incorrect Tools

Severe and irreparable damage can occur if a gardener is using incorrect tools for their bonsai maintenance and care. Every bonsai owner should own a pair of high-quality bonsai scissors. These are a specialty tool created for properly pruning bonsais with as little damage as possible. They are made to cut through wires which are supporting your tree as well as branches. If you utilize regular scissors for these tasks, it will end up damaging your bonsai and likely cause scarring.

You will also need to have branch cutters, wire pliers and wire cutters the more mature your bonsai becomes. These are all tools which will need to be specifically for bonsai tree care and the maintenance of your tree will grow more complex as the tree matures.

Be sure to care for your tools and keep them in the best shape possible. To remove rust or dirt from the blades, you can use a product known as Clean Mate. To keep the tools sharp, purchase a grindstone as branches and leaves need to be sliced cleanly. This cannot happen with a dull pair of scissors or cutters and will, in turn, damage your bonsai.

Action Steps if your Bonsai is Dying

If you have found yourself where your tree is suffering and dying, there is some hope if you have caught the symptoms in time. There are guidelines to try to revive your bonsai tree. First, you need to know the type of tree and if it is an indoor or outdoor bonsai. This will help you to determine the specific needs and care for your particular tree. If you have not already, educate yourself on the particular type of bonsai you own as some variations have niche needs which may be the cause of the tree dying.

Ensure that you have followed the guidelines for the location, fertilization, and watering of your plant. If not, adjust accordingly. Sometimes this alone will bring the bonsai back to life when it is in its ideal environment to thrive.

Keep in mind that bonsais are better kept in temperatures greater than 20° Fahrenheit (-6° Celsius) during the winter time. You can bring them inside to a warmer place as the bonsai does not need sunlight while in a dormant state. You may notice the foliage turn brown, but they will become green again during the spring when they are set back outside.

Make sure that your bonsai tree is supposed to be indoors or outdoors. As an example, the popular Juniper bonsais are an outdoor plant. If placed indoors, the foliage will start to yellow and fall off the tree. Because most of the indoor bonsais are sub-tropical trees, they require abundant light. Some new owners may think for this reason that it is best to keep their bonsai outdoors. However, the guidelines for each variety must be followed.

Once you are knowledgeable about the particular care for your variety of bonsai tree, continue to follow those guidelines as this is the best thing that can be done for your tree going forward to revive and thrive.

Conclusion (planting your own bonsai)

I would like to thank you once again for downloading this book.

Bonsai is an art and, like any skill, you can learn this as well. There are a couple of critical yet straightforward steps that you should follow to create your bonsai. Start by selecting seed to grow a tree of your choice. You can either start with a seed or purchase a pre-bonsai sapling. Once you do this, you have to select a container for your bonsai. After these two steps, it is all about pruning and caring for the plant. You have to water the plant regularly and give it all the necessary fertilizers to ensure that it thrives. You are the caregiver, and you are the only one that can make sure that your plant thrives. So, take utmost care of it.

Now that you are equipped with everything you need to know to grow your bonsai, the next step is to get started. You need to be quite patient and nourish your plant into a beautiful bonsai tree. All the effort you put into it will undoubtedly be worth your while. All the best!